Contents

GW00818865

Photographs supplied by G.F. Brookes

Foreword

The sport of sub aqua has grown during the past 35 years to take its place alongside other major recreational pastimes, the challenge of new horizons and adventure giving it a particular appeal. To man, who is so thoroughly adapted for life on land and to breathing air, the sea is an alien element. Even to travel on it involves dangers, risks of shipwreck, drowning, fears of the unknown. Swimming and particularly underwater swimming, involves overcoming these fears and learning to master this element.

There have been great developments since the early days when a few dedicated enthusiasts learned to use unfamiliar equipment, overcame difficulties and problems and gained experience from which to develop a sound and effective training programme for the many sports divers who were to follow them. The often turbulent waters round the British coasts frown on the foolish adventurer,

and experience has taught training and diving procedures that place safety above all else. In consequence, these methods have been adopted the world over.

Along with the ability to penetrate under water has developed a knowledge of the world below the waves; books have been written, photographs taken, conferences organised, scientific work undertaken, wrecks found and given careful archaeological excavation. History is being opened to us.

Although the sport is a strenuous one, anyone who can swim and is physically fit can take part, but as with any adventurous activity it is important that the correct techniques are learned. This book sets these out in a clear and concise form, both for 'snorkel diving' with fins, mask and snorkel tube, and for 'aqualung diving' with compressed air breathing apparatus.

As a result of the formation of sub-aqua clubs, thousands now have their

own fins, mask and snorkel tube, learn to use them with a recognised club and enjoy this fascinating sport around the coast or in inland lakes and waters.

Of the several reasons why beginners at underwater swimming should join a club devoted to this sport are the enjoyment they will get in meeting other enthusiasts and the assistance afforded to their own training by these enthusiasts' example, advice and experience.

Throughout this book stress has been laid on the personal safety of the diver and particularly on diving at all times with a companion. Within a club such companions will be found.

For those who are interested in taking up this sport there are branches of the British Sub-Aqua Club situated throughout the British Isles and in many other countries, details of which can be obtained by writing to the BSAC, 16 Upper Woburn Place, London WC1H OQW.

The underwater world

Fig. 1 The underwater world

Life on the world began in the seas – probably in the tidal zone where millions of years ago there first occurred favourable accumulations of chemicals, sunlight and water movements; from the tidal waters there later emerged the different plants and creatures which evolved to inhabit the land areas.

On entering these waters the underwater swimmer sees a world which is full of fascination, strange, almost silent. It is inhabited by innumerable creatures, some large, some small and some so minute that their presence is only detectable by the green colour their myriad bodies impart to the water. The sea creatures live in a vast world covering seven-tenths of the earth's surface. Its depth varies from the several miles of the deep ocean floors to the shallower waters surrounding the continental land masses, but it is only within the first thirty metres where sunlight can penetrate that vegetation is abundant. Here grow all types of sea weeds and marine plants; and where this plant life is prolific there live a multitude of animals, sheltering within it, eating and being eaten; fish of all shapes, sizes, and colours (Fig. 1). With the advent of the aqualung, man has become part of the underwater world and can observe it at first hand. (Please note that where divers are referred to as 'he' in this book, this should be taken as 'he or she' where appropriate.)

Despite their vast size, the resources of the seas are not inexhaustible. Fish, for example, can be depleted by overexploitation; pollution, produced by sewage, chemical waste or oil spillage, can profoundly affect life conditions in offshore waters.

The land and sea together form a fruitful partnership, which must be maintained by conservation and control. Because he has entry into both these environments the underwater swimmer can play an important part in maintaining our planet as a suitable place in which to live.

The two great problems

There are two great problems that face anyone who ventures under water. The first is how to obtain a supply of air, for we can only live a short time without it, and the other is coping with difficulties caused by the pressure effects on the body of the surrounding water.

Air supply

For many years the only practical means of staying alive under water was to use the 'standard diving suit'. In this the diver was virtually tied to the surface by his air line which was connected to a pump operated by his attendants at the surface. Although the wartime 'frogmen' had a self-contained diving apparatus needing no line to the surface, this apparatus was complicated to use and employed pure oxygen, which is dangerous to breathe. Only after the war was there developed an apparatus safe for use by the sports diver. This is also self-contained. A

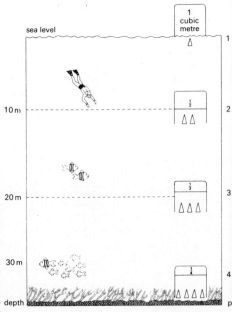

Fig. 2 Changes of pressure with depth

cylinder of compressed air with a demand valve supplies the diver with air only as required giving him freedom of movement. The 'aqualung', as this apparatus is called, has opened up the underwater world to thousands of adventurers.

Pressure effects

At the surface of the earth a person is subjected to atmospheric pressure caused by the weight of the air above him. This normal pressure is almost exactly equal to the metric measurement of pressure called a 'bar', although it is sometimes referred to as an 'at.' (for atmosphere).

As a diver descends into the water he experiences an increasing pressure due to the additional weight of the water above him. For every 10 metres of depth, the pressure increases by 1 bar. Thus at sea level the pressure is 1 bar; at 10 metres the weight of the water is equivalent to a pressure of 1 bar so the total pressure (that due to the air and the water) is 2 bar. Similarly at 20 metres it is 3 bar, and at 30 metres 4 bar, and so on. The reason that these greatly increasing pressures do not squash the body is that they are acting equally from all sides, including inside because the air pressure in the lungs is maintained at the same pressure as the water outside.

Unlike water, air changes its volume when it is compressed (Fig. 2). If a cubic metre of air at the surface is taken in a container open to the water pressure, it will be reduced in volume to half a cubic metre at a depth of 10 metres. In the same way that the pressure is increased with depth the volume of air is decreased; at 20 metres it will be one third while at 30 metres it will only be a quarter of the volume it was at the surface. This relationship of the decrease in volume of air with the increase in pressure is known as Boyle's Law.

A reverse process takes place when ascending; the volume of air in the container when it is at 30 metres will increase as it is brought up, until at the surface it is four times the volume it was 30 metres down.

These changes are of great importance to divers using a snorkel tube as well as to aqualung divers for reasons that are explained later in this book.

Learning to dive

This book describes the equipment and techniques for diving but it can only complement, not replace, practical coaching. This can be obtained in three main ways: by joining a diving club which holds regular training meetings, by receiving instruction at a special diving school, or by attending a course at a holiday diving centre.

The beginner will normally receive initial training in a swimming pool or sheltered water, first with the basic equipment of fins, mask and snorkel, then progressing to the use of the aqualung in open water.

Basic equipment

There are many different types and makes of fins, masks and snorkels available to the diver and the choice depends on their correct fitting and personal preference. An understanding of their function and limitations will help the novice to make a satisfactory choice.

Mask

The primary purpose of the mask is to enable the diver to see clearly under water. Normally when swimming under water everything is vague because water next to the eyes upsets their focussing properties. A mask (Fig. 3) solves this problem by putting the eyes back into air, their natural environment, and so restoring their normal functioning. The diver can now see clearly everything under water that is within his range of vision, the former vague outlines coming sharply into focus.

Although the diver can see clearly, however, he does not see things under water in their actual size. This is because the flat face of the mask acts with the water as a magnifying lens which makes objects look one-third bigger than they actually are and also appear to be only three-quarters of their actual distance away (Fig. 4). This may seem strange at first and cause the diver to misjudge the size and distance of things he tries to pick up. The apparently large crab he collects

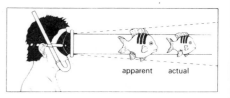

apparent   actual

Fig. 4 Things look larger and nearer under water

from the sea bed (with some difficulty, because it seems closer than it actually is) may well turn out to be quite small when he brings it to the surface. With experience, however, the diver very soon learns to make mental adjustments for these effects and he need worry about them no longer.

In choosing a mask the diver must get one which covers both the eyes and nose. As the diver goes deeper the pressure of the water surrounding him increases. This causes the volume of the air in the mask to decrease and it will tend to collapse onto his face. In order to prevent discomfort and to restore the mask to its proper shape the diver must breathe out some air through his nose into the mask to

Fig. 3 Two types of mask

equalise the pressure. After a little experience the diver learns to do this automatically. On the way up, the excess air pressure will escape around the edge of the mask, so the diver does not need to do anything special about it. In consequence goggles which cover the eyes only and cannot be pressurised through the nose are not suitable for underwater swimming. Also masks with built-in snorkel tubes should not be used as they can be dangerous.

The most important thing about the mask is that it should fit properly, and not leak under water. This can easily be tested on the surface. Without using the straps, place the mask in position on the face, suck in through the nose and the mask should stay in position on its own without air leaking in. If it does this it should be a good fit for the diver. It is essential that the mask is designed to allow the nose to be pinched from the outside while being worn, to assist 'ear clearing' when going down, which is explained later in this book. It is also a desirable feature that the mask has a faceplate of unbreakable glass, rather than of plastic, which tends to mist up easily. The faceplate should be held securely in place by the mask moulding or by a securing band.

If while snorkel diving the mask does get some water in it, the correct way to clear it out is to return to the surface, tread water vertically and lift one lower corner so that the water will run out (Fig. 5). Do not remove the mask to clear it as this not only takes a long time, but while you are putting it on again more water will probably get in.

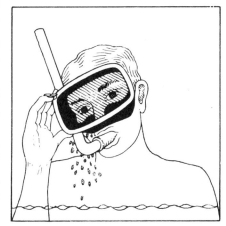

Fig. 5 Mask clearing at the surface

Fins

Man's arms and legs are not adapted for propulsion in the water and in ordinary swimming both have to be used to keep afloat. However, with the use of fins on the feet there is so much extra power that there is no need to use the arms at all. In fact, while swimming under water it is better not to use the arms to swim, but rather to keep them free for carrying or picking up things as required.

There are a number of different patterns of fins to choose from. Very large fins put a big strain on the leg muscles and the beginner is well advised to select fins which have a stiffened blade with a medium surface size and a shoe part of soft rubber. Some fin designs include slots in the blade which reduce the finning effort required. A comfortable fit is important. If the fins are too tight they may cause cramp, while if too loose they may come off in use.

There are two main styles: those with a heel strap, which can also be adjustable; and those with a full heel like a shoe (Fig. 6). The heel strap leaves the heel unprotected but the full-heeled types usually have the toes exposed. Floating types are of no special advantage as a well-fitting fin should not come off in use. If there is no exact size available it is preferable to get fins slightly too large and to wear socks or the rubber boots of a diving suit in them.

Swimming with the aid of basic equipment is called 'finning' because of the essential difference between it and ordinary swimming. The underwater swimmer is at home in the water; he should move slowly and gracefully on the surface and below the water, with the minimum of effort, by the use of the fins alone. There is no need to use the arms to get along – in fact they are more of a hindrance than a help if used this way, particularly while under water. They can be used initially to help in making a dive and subsequently while under water to aid change of direction, but at other times they are better kept at the sides or held out straight in front.

Finning should be a calm movement; no splashing on the surface; no racing furiously up and down a swimming pool as this can be dangerous both to the finner and other users of the pool. Moreover, this can soon lead to exhaustion and consequent risk of drowning. Thus one of the fundamentals the underwater swimmer must learn is that finning is a calm, controlled, and relaxed activity. When the simple technique of finning has been mastered the diver will find himself free to observe all that goes on under water.

Snorkel tube

While the mask enables the diver to see under water and the fins give him considerable power for swimming, neither of them enable him to remain below the surface, for he must come up and lift his head out of the water every time he needs to take a breath. The snorkel tube solves this difficulty. By lying on the surface with the face in the water and breathing through the snorkel, the diver can watch the underwater scene continuously. When he wishes to fin down he can just hold his breath and dive, coming to the surface again when he needs to take another breath. This ability constitutes the art of snorkel diving.

Snorkel tubes are usually made of rubber or plastic. The simplest type consists of a 'J' shaped tube, open at

◄Fig. 6 Two types of fin
Fig. 7 Two types of snorkel tube►

one end and fitted with a mouthpiece at the other. Some tubes have the upper end slightly curved over the diver's head (Fig. 7). The bend at the mouthpiece end is made so that the tube will project out of the water at the side of the diver's head when swimming on the surface face downwards. The mouthpiece should be placed in the mouth with the rubber flange between the lips and the gums. The two small rubber lugs should be gripped lightly between the teeth to prevent the mouthpiece coming out of the mouth. The length of the tube should be such that it projects only a few centimetres above the head. If it is either too narrow or too long, breathing through it will be difficult or impossible, and if too short water may splash in.

In order to prevent the tube from being lost, or tilting backwards into the water, or pulling at the mouthpiece, it should be tucked between the mask strap and the head just in front of the ear. Alternatively it may be fixed to the mask strap by means of binding or a special rubber moulding which slips over the tube and goes round the mask strap.

Fig. 8 Clearing the snorkel tube

After a dive, or at any other time when water may have got into the tube, it is an easy matter to clear it out again. With the face held downwards just give a short strong blow through the tube and the water will be blown out of the open end above the surface (Fig. 8). If there are a few drops left in the tube it is still possible to take a breath in carefully and then blow out these last drops with a second try.

Some types of tube are fitted with a valve at the mouthpiece for self-draining, which aids clearing. However, if the lungs are empty when surfacing, it is not possible then to blow out. In this case fin vertically at the surface, remove the tube from the mouth and turn it sideways so as to prevent any water that is running out from jetting into the mouth. The diver can then take a breath, replace the mouthpiece and clear the tube with a short blow.

Snorkel tubes that are fitted with various water-excluding types of valve may add false confidence to a nervous beginner: their use can be dangerous because they may fail or impede the flow of air.

The snorkel tube is an essential part of the snorkel diver's equipment and is a great aid to safety. If tired or on a long swim he can lie effortless in the water to recover his breath or rest, whereas without it he would constantly have to lift his head out of the water to breathe.

Never dive without your snorkel tube. Even when diving with an aqualung, always take a snorkel tube which you can then use at the end of the dive if low on air.

9

Basic training

The novice should start his training under someone already competent. This will be a great aid to learning and is also an important safety precaution. The simplest way to do this is to join a reputable diving club with the use of a swimming pool where training is given.

The beginner should get used to the equipment. Try fitting it on dry land first – each item in turn – and then try it out, preferably in the safe waters of a swimming pool. In order to prevent the mask misting up when worn, spit on to the inside of the faceplate, rub round and then rinse out in the water. Fit the mask over the face, adjust the strap – not too tight – and breathe through the mouth. Next place the snorkel tube up the side of the mask strap in front of the ear and put the mouthpiece into the mouth. You will find that you will need to breathe more deeply than normally because of the extra air in the snorkel tube which has to be taken in and out with each breath. Rinse the fins in the water so that they will slip on the feet easily and fit them.

Now get slowly into the shallow end of the swimming pool. Never jump or dive in – you will probably lose your mask if you do so and may hurt some other person already in the water. Get used to breathing through the snorkel tube and then, while still breathing through it, crouch down and put your face just below the surface. The open end of the tube should be out of the water. Do this as often as necessary until you are quite happy about breathing with the face in the water and look around you to discover how clearly you can now see under water.

Next, hold on to the side of the pool and stretch out fully on the surface with the face just below the water. Continue to breathe through the snor-

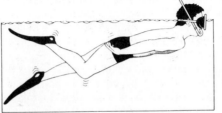

Fig. 9 Finning at the surface

kel and practise the fin stroke with the legs. The stroke is a long, slow crawl action performed mainly from the hips. The legs should be relaxed and only slightly flexed at the knees and the toes pointing. Avoid a cycling action from the knee joints as this reduces the power available for propulsion.

When you have got the feel of this stroke, commence finning across the bath. Try not to let the fins break the surface of the water and cause splashing. The disadvantages of this are, first, that a lot of power is lost, and, second, that it will frighten away fish when you are in open waters. It is avoided by lying out full length on the surface and letting your body droop a little into the water (Fig. 9). Your hands should be kept at your sides. When you are quite confident with this finning you can practise in deeper water.

Do not use the new power of your fins for fast and energetic finning, or you will soon become exhausted. Keep your movements controlled and relaxed.

Snorkel diving

Much can be seen, and much enjoyment obtained, by finning on the surface and watching the underwater scene; but to enter more fully into the underwater world the experienced snorkel diver will spend some time below the surface. To do this, further techniques have to be learnt. The simplest way to get below is by means of the 'jack-knife dive' (Fig. 10). Stretch out fully on the surface with the hands in front. Take a breath and hold it. Bend downwards at the waist to bring head and body under water and the legs parallel with the surface. Straighten out the body so that the feet and legs are almost upright out of the water. The weight of the legs will then force the body downwards until the fins are below the surface. In order to assist this downward movement the hands can be pulled back to the sides in a breast stroke action. Not until the fins are fully below the water should they be used for finning, as otherwise an untidy splashing will result.

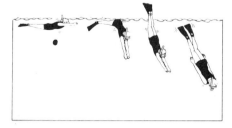

Fig. 10 Jack knife dive

Once under water the same finning stroke as on the surface should be used. It will be found that finning under water is easier and the action smoother than at the surface. Proceed calmly, parallel to the surface, for a short distance, then look up to see that you will not come up under another swimmer and surface. Keeping the face held downwards in the water clear the snorkel tube with a short blow and carry on finning. Practise this until you are quite competent.

Of course, during this training water will get into the snorkel tube and possibly also into the mask, but by following the drills outlined it is an easy matter to clear it out again and it should present no difficulties.

There is, however, one further drill that should be mastered – to be able to breathe through the snorkel tube even though there is water in the mask that is covering the nose. This can be practised by letting a little water into the mask or by finning on the surface without the mask and keeping the face in the water while still breathing through the snorkel.

At first you may find this very difficult to achieve. The way to learn is to imagine that you are closing the nose, not at the nostrils, but at the back. Keep still in the water and attempt to breathe through the snorkel. When you can do this, then try finning along the surface. As this is a very important safety drill you should definitely attempt to master it as soon as you can.

Breath holding

Everyone knows that we must breathe to live, but the reasons for this and the actions of breathing by the body are very complex. In simple terms it can be said that all the functions of the body – to live, grow, think, move – require not only food but also oxygen. This oxygen is obtained from the air we breathe.

We breathe in air which contains about 20 per cent oxygen and 80 per cent nitrogen; and we breathe out stale air which contains about 16 per cent oxygen, 4 per cent carbon dioxide and 80 per cent nitrogen (Fig. 11). Some of the oxygen has been changed into carbon dioxide by the body, while the nitrogen has performed no active function, but has passed through the body unchanged. However, as explained later (pp. 31–2), the effects of nitrogen on deeper dives are of vital importance.

The oxygen in the air is taken into the body through the nose or mouth and to the lungs where it passes into the blood which carries it to every part of the body. The blood also brings back the carbon dioxide from the body to the lungs where it is breathed out. The more active you are, the more oxygen you use up in the body and therefore the more carbon dioxide you have to get rid of in order to maintain the correct amounts of oxygen and carbon dioxide that the body needs.

An understanding of these facts is very important for the underwater swimmer, particularly as the body can only live for a very short time if it is deprived of the necessary air for breathing.

When snorkel diving the breath has to be held all the time the diver is below the surface thus limiting the time of the dive. However, with proper techniques and practice, the duration of the dive can be extended in the following manner. If out of breath through exertion or a previous dive, rest easily on the surface, breathing through the snorkel tube until normal relaxed breathing is regained. Then take two or three deep breaths, concentrating on exhaling to the full extent so as to get rid of as much stale air from the lungs as possible. Breathe in and dive. On surfacing, clear the snorkel and once more rest or fin easily while regaining your breath.

It is very dangerous to overbreathe, that is, to continue with deep breathing before a dive, as so much of the carbon dioxide will be removed from the body that while holding your breath you may use up oxygen to the extent that you become unconscious under water, with fatal results. This can occur because it is an increasing amount of carbon dioxide in the lungs rather than a lack of oxygen that produces a desire to breathe and controls the depth and rate of breathing. Thus **only take two or three deep breaths** before a dive – never overbreathe.

The duration of a snorkel dive depends on how long you can safely hold your breath, and this to some extent

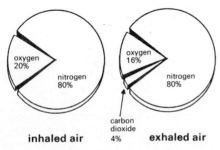

oxygen
20%

nitrogen
80%

oxygen
16%

nitrogen
80%

carbon
dioxide
4%

inhaled air   **exhaled air**

Fig. 11 The air we breathe

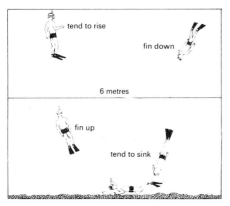

Fig. 12 Change of buoyancy with depth

determines how deep you can go, for you must always allow sufficient time to surface before you need to breathe again. Thus you should only increase the depth of your diving gradually as, with practice, you become able to stay longer under water.

However, there are other factors which also limit the depth you can attain. As you go down, the air in the lungs is compressed by the water pressure. This reduces the size of the lungs and the change is taken up by the flexibility of the chest walls and by movements of the diaphragm as in breathing. However, if you were to go too deep – beyond the considerable depth of 30 metres – the size of the lungs could not be reduced further by this method and serious damage to them would result.

The change of size of the lungs with depth also changes the diver's buoyancy. With a full breath most people are slightly buoyant on the surface, which means that they will not sink unless they make a deliberate effort to do so. However, at about 6 metres depth the reduced volume of their lungs, due to the effect of the increased pressure, makes them slightly heavier than water and they will sink. It follows that you probably need to fin down to 6 metres, and will then tend to sink, whereas you will need additional effort to fin up again to 6 metres before you become buoyant once more, which will assist your finning towards the surface (Fig. 12).

For these reasons deep snorkel diving involves unnecessary risks and should therefore be avoided. The following should also be taken into account.

The ears

Another factor that may limit the depth you can reach is the effect of the water pressure on your ears (Fig. 13). As you go down, the increasing water pressure pushes from the outside on to the ear drum and, if a corresponding pressure is not maintained on its other side, pain will result. This will be followed by a burst ear drum if the pain is ignored and the descent continued. In order to equalise the pressures on the ear drum, some of the air in the lungs

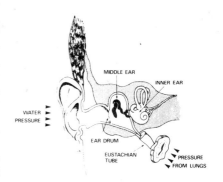

Fig. 13 The ear

must flow through the 'Eustachian tube' to the middle ear. This can be achieved by going through the action of swallowing, which opens up the Eustachian tube to allow air to pass. Normally, the tube will open fairly easily, but if there is some obstruction, such as can result from a cold, the air will not pass and the descent must be stopped.

It is often possible to assist ears that are difficult to clear by pinching the nose and blowing gently, when the ears will be felt to 'pop' as the pressures equalise. Only masks that are specially designed to enable the nose to be pinched from outside the mask while under water are suitable for diving.

When first taking up diving, some trouble may be experienced in 'clearing the ears', but with practice and constant use the Eustachian tubes will open more easily. As soon as you commence a dive you should start clearing your ears and continue to do so throughout the dive as you go down. Fortunately, little trouble is experienced on the ascent as the excess pressure in the ears will force the Eustachian tube open and the air will flow away.

Because of the need to equalise pressures and to avoid damage to the ear drums it is essential that the ears are kept free. For this reason **never use ear plugs** or wear a tight fitting hood to a diving suit that blocks off the ears from contact with the pressure of the surrounding water.

Fitness

Anyone who is physically fit and can swim should be able to dive. It is, however, a strenuous sport which requires acquisition of correct techniques and achievement of competent performance. Regular training in the safe waters of a swimming pool is the best way to do this as well as to maintain efficiency during the winter months when, perhaps, you may not be able to dive in open water.

You would be well advised, also, to have a medical examination before taking up diving to confirm that you are fit to do so. A sound heart and healthy lungs are essential and there should be no condition, such as high blood pressure, epilepsy or diabetes, which might produce unconsciousness

in the water. Any blockage of the Eustachian tubes, which would prevent equalising pressures on the ear drums, will preclude diving. Thus, people with constant colds, hay fever, ear or sinus infections should not take up diving. Even if you can normally clear the ears easily an attempt to do so when you have a cold may force the infection into the middle ear or sinuses with consequent unpleasant results. For this reason **never dive when suffering from a cold**.

If you have not had a recent medical check, or if at any time you have doubts about your health or physical condition, consult your doctor. Most diving clubs and diving schools insist that their members have an initial chest X-ray, and medical examinations at regular intervals to ensure that they dive only if they are fit to do so. Even if you are generally fit you should not dive if you are temporally unwell or overtired as this may adversely affect your safety in the water or the enjoyment of your dive.

Open water

For the diver who has learnt the techniques of snorkel diving in a swimming pool there should be no difficulties in carrying them out correctly in open water; and he has the advantage that he has overcome all the problems associated with the beginner under conditions where they could easily be observed by a companion and corrected.

But the need for a companion does not end when training is completed.

When diving in open water, particularly in the sea, always dive with someone else, and keep with him, so that in the event of any trouble assistance is always at hand. After each dive look round to check that your companion diver is still with you, as it is surprising how far you can drift apart even during the time of one snorkel dive.

When sea diving it is wise to know the local conditions and to respect the sea and its ways. Avoid strong tides and currents and rough water. Entering the sea also has its problems; make sure you can get out again. The most interesting underwater scenery will be found round rocks where seaweed grows and fish congregate; not over the relatively barren stretches of flat sand. Therefore it is preferable to enter the sea from a sandy beach adjacent to a rocky outcrop.

Fins, that help so greatly when swimming, make walking difficult and it is preferable to put them on at the edge of the water and to walk in back-

Fig. 14 Open water snorkelling

15

wards until it is deep enough for finning, or, where possible, to enter from a rock into deeper, sheltered water. Remember that with fins you can go a long way in a very short time, so take care that you don't get too far away from the shore to return safely. In addition it is a good practice to have someone watching you from the shore who can render assistance if need be.

Before diving in open water it is as well to know the simple treatments and first aid for diving accidents. Cuts and scratches occur very easily under water as the skin is soft and rocks with their accompanying barnacles and shellfish are often sharp. Moreover, pain which is produced in air from damage to the skin is reduced or lacking when in water so that quite deep cuts may go unnoticed until after leaving the water. Abrasions should be given first aid treatment by being cleaned and covered. If they are deep you should not enter the water again until they are healed, as infection or troublesome salt water sores may develop. Of course, anything serious should have proper medical treatment as soon as possible.

Aqualung diving

The diver with mask, fins and snorkel tube can penetrate the underwater world and see its beauties, but is limited to a series of glimpses and to a shallow depth by the need to return after a short interval to the surface to breathe. In order to have adequate time to see, observe and possibly photograph the underwater scene and creatures he must be able to stay down for a longer period. This the aqualung enables him to do, in effect by replacing the snorkel tube with a supply of air which the diver carries with him.

However, using an aqualung does present problems of its own, mainly associated with the duration of the diver's air supply and the changing pressures surrounding him as he fins up and down in the water. Unlike snorkel diving where the diver **must** hold his breath under water, the diver with an aqualung should **never** hold his breath, but carry on breathing naturally all the time, taking particular care when ascending because the pressurised air in his lungs will expand on the ascent and must be breathed out freely or lung damage will result. It is very important to understand these problems and to learn how to use the aqualung correctly. The simplest and most sensible way to do this is to join a reputable diving club or school.

Principles

If a snorkel diver, in an attempt to breathe further below the surface, tried to use a longer tube at even one metre of depth he would be quite unable to do so. This is because the lungs and chest walls are designed to function with equalised pressures, inside and out. The air in the snorkel tube would be at surface pressure while the outside pressure of the water would be increasing as he went down. It is therefore essential that the air supplied to the diver is at the same pressure as that of the surrounding water. Even a slight difference corresponding to that of only a

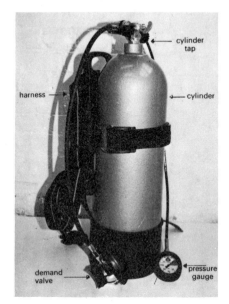

Fig. 15 The aqualung

few centimetres of water will make breathing extremely difficult. To provide air at the correct pressure is the secret of the aqualung.

The aqualung (Fig. 15) consists of two main parts: (i) a cylinder fitted with an ON/OFF tap, containing compressed air that will supply the diver with his needs for a period under water, which is connected to (ii) a demand valve that controls the flow of air from the cylinder through a mouthpiece as a means of conveying this air to the diver. The cylinder is the largest and heaviest part of the equipment and is carried in a harness on the diver's back.

The harness should be comfortable to wear and should not impede the diver's movements in any way. It is important that it has a simple and reliable method of fastening which can be easily operated by the diver even while in the water.

The demand valve is the heart of the apparatus. It consists basically of a flexible diaphragm, one side of which is in contact with the water and the other with the air as supplied to the diver from the cylinder (Fig. 16).

When the diver breathes in, the suction created moves the diaphragm and causes it to open an air inlet valve so as to admit more air from the cylinder. The fact that one side of the diaphragm is in contact with the water ensures that the air on its other side is maintained at the same pressure as that of the water. When the inhalation is complete the diaphragm reverts to its original position, stopping the flow of air.

Ease of breathing depends on two things; the mechanical efficiency of the demand valve and the position of its diaphragm relative to the centre of pressure of the diver's lungs. The further the demand valve is away from this position, the greater will be the effort required to breathe and the more this effort will vary with the diver's attitude in the water.

When the diver exhales, the stale air is liberated into the water through a non-return valve. This valve must be placed at the same level as the diaphragm. If it were at a higher level in

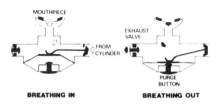

Fig. 16 Principles of the demand valve

the water air would flow away continuously from the diaphragm through the exhaust valve; whereas if it were lower no air would be lost, but the effort of exhalation would be increased unnecessarily.

Thus the demand valve not only supplies air at the correct pressure for breathing, but also provides it only when needed – that is on demand – and hence is economical on the use of air and, providing the demand valve is of an efficient design, will continue to supply the diver at any depth as long as there is air left in the cylinder.

Demand valves

Most demand valves consist of two stages connected together by a medium pressure air hose. The final stage includes the mouthpiece and needs to be relatively small and light in construction, otherwise it will be difficult to keep in place in the mouth.

The exhaust outlet is a water excluding valve so situated that the bubbles of exhaled air pass by the side of the diver's face, and do not normally obstruct his vision. In order that water can be cleared out of the mouthpiece

the demand valve is made so that the diaphragm can be operated by hand to give a large flow of air. This is usually referred to as the 'purge button'.

A preliminary reducing valve is mounted on the cylinder, which limits the air in the medium pressure hose to a constant level above that of the surrounding water. Thus the breathing characteristics of the demand valve do not change while the air is being used up from the cylinder.

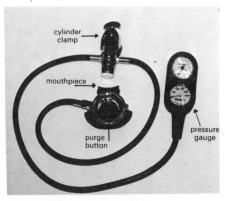

Fig. 17 Demand valve

This preliminary stage usually has a high pressure take off point for connection of a cylinder contents pressure gauge. It may also have one or more medium pressure take offs for supplying air to special equipment such as a second mouthpiece stage, lifejacket, or for dry suit inflation.

Before purchasing a demand valve it is important to ensure it is of sound design because the fact that it may give easy breathing at or near the surface does not necessarily mean that it will supply adequate air at depth.

Air cylinders

Aqualung cylinders for use in diving are made to a stringent specification for their use in the rigorous environment of sea water and because of the high pressures of air involved. They may be made from steel or aluminium. A tap is fitted to the neck of the cylinder to control the on and off of the air supply (Fig. 17).

The time you can stay under water is limited by the amount of air in the aqualung cylinder at the commencement of the dive. This in turn depends on the size of the cylinder (or cylinders if equipment with more than one cylinder is being used) and the maximum pressure of the air with which the cylinder has been charged. A common pressure to which cylinders are charged in Great Britain is 200 bar, or sometimes more depending on the cylinder construction. At this pressure a considerable amount of air has been compressed into the cylinder which would be extremely dangerous if it should burst.

For this reason it is important to treat cylinders with care and to ensure that they are not weakened by damage or corrosion. Regulations are in force that require cylinders – both steel and aluminium – to be internally inspected each year and specially tested every two years. If this is done and care taken of them there should be little risk of trouble.

The amount of air that a cylinder can hold when charged to its maximum pressure is called its capacity. This is the same as the volume that the air occupied before it was compressed into the cylinders. A common capacity of cylinders for aqualungs is 2000 litres (Fig. 18).

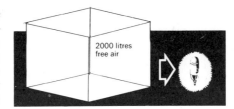

Fig. 18 Cylinder capacity

Air endurance

On average a diver who is moderately exerting himself breathes in and out 30 litres of air a minute at the same pressure as that of the surrounding water. This means that he uses twice as much air at 10 metres as he does at the surface, three times as much at 20 metres and so on. In consequence a diver using a 2000 litre cylinder would be able to remain about one hour just below the surface, but if he descended to 10 metres his time would be reduced to 30 minutes, while at 30 metres it would be only 15 minutes. Thus the demand valve has to supply a greater amount of air when the diver is at depth than when he is near the surface and in consequence its efficiency at depth is important if the diver is not to encounter a restriction to his breathing.

Not only the depth, but also the diver's exertion, cold water and excitement increase the amount of air breathed and thereby reduce the time of a dive. To obtain the best endurance, therefore, a diver must breathe efficiently with long deep breaths, move slowly and economically, have adequate protective clothing and full confidence in his equipment.

As a result of these variable factors some more positive indication is necessary to the diver that his air supply is running low than the time he has been in the water, although it is good practice to plan your dive by working

Fig. 19 Pressure gauge

out beforehand the depth you will be at and how long you are likely to be able to remain there. For a check on the air supplies, a pressure gauge connected directly to the cylinder is the most accurate method (Fig. 19) and enables the diver to see at any time exactly how much air remains. Some cylinders are fitted with a reserve valve which prevents a small percentage of the air from being used. When the diver finds his air supply exhausted, he can open the reserve, which should contain sufficient air for him to surface.

It is important to check the pressure gauge regularly during a dive – particularly at depth – as little warning may be obtained that the air supply is getting low by an increasing resistance to breathing.

Once empty, cylinders can be recharged with compressed air from a suitable compressor which delivers air for breathing. It is important that the cylinders are not charged beyond their maximum working pressure and that the air supplied is both pure and free from moisture. Only firms supplying medically pure air should be allowed to fill your cylinders.

Approximate air endurance of a 2000 litre cylinder	
DEPTH (metres)	MINUTES
Surface	60
5	40
10	30
15	24
20	20
25	17
30	15
35	13
40	12
45	11
50	10

By joining a diving club that has a compressor you can overcome recharging problems.

Weight belts

The snorkel diver without wetsuit is usually slightly buoyant on the surface, but the buoyancy of the aqualung diver is considerably influenced by the equipment he is wearing. The ideal condition is to be neutrally buoyant, that is to say the diver will neither rise nor sink unless he deliberately makes himself do so. At the best this can only be approximately achieved as the amount of air in his lungs and in the cylinder will affect it. The weight of air in a fully charged 2000 litre cylinder is approximately 2 kilograms.

Thus allowance has to be made for the weight of the aqualung in the water. Some cylinders will float at least when empty, and some weight has to be carried by the diver to counteract this; and due to the greater density of sea water more weight has to be carried in it than when diving in fresh water. The weight required will vary from a few kilograms up to about 10 kilograms or more if a diving suit is being worn. As the diver can only tolerate a variation from neutral buoyancy of about one kilogram if he is to be able to fin easily, it can be seen that the correct adjustment of buoyancy is most important.

The correct way to determine the weight required is to enter the water definitely underweighted and then to add weights gradually until when just below the surface and without other movement you will sink when you exhale and rise when you inhale. The weights are usually of lead and carried on a separate quick-release weight-belt round the waist (Fig. 20).

Achievement of neutral buoyancy can make or mar a dive. It is dangerous to be too heavy and difficult to keep the fins from stirring up sand or mud from the bottom. If too light the diver will experience considerable discomfort and will expend much wasted effort in trying to keep down.

It is of vital importance for safety that all weights are attached by an efficient quick release. Weight-belts should be worn over other equipment so that they can be jettisoned at once in an emergency. The diver should

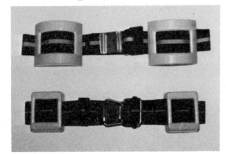

Fig. 20 Quick-release weight belts

always check the correct functioning of the quick-release before diving and make sure that he can operate it without difficulty while in the water by feel alone. **Always use an efficient quick-release.**

Diving suits

Water can absorb a large quantity of heat and when flowing over a diver it rapidly conducts away heat from the surface of his body. Although it may be possible to remain in warm waters for some hours without protection, the loss of body heat will eventually reach a state where it becomes dangerous to remain longer in the water. When diving in cold waters such as those usually found round the coasts of the British Isles heat is very quickly lost from the body. After a short time, depending on the temperature of the water, the diver becomes so chilled that the dive has to be discontinued. Thus, for the sake of comfort and safety as well as to increase the time of the dive, some protection against the cold is necessary. In warm or tropical waters simple protection is obtained by wearing a close-fitting woollen garment such as a pull-

over in the water. This minimises the flow of water over the diver's skin and thereby reduces the amount of heat which is conducted away by the water.

In colder waters much greater heat insulation is achieved by wearing a specially made garment of expended synthetic rubber, close fitting to the skin – called a **wet suit** (Fig. 21). Although water can get into the suit, its close fitting nature almost eliminates the water flow so that it soon warms up to near body temperature. A wet suit is very comfortable to wear, but in order to be fully effective it must be a good fit and as such it is usually kept as a personal item of diving equipment. Some wet suits have additional seals at the ankles, wrists and neck to exclude water from entering.

The good insulation property of these suits rests on the incorporation of a large number of small bubbles in the manufacture of the rubber. These bubbles give to the suit a degree of buoyancy that the diver has to counteract by carrying weights with him in order to be able to descend into the water. As he goes down, however, increasing pressure of the surrounding

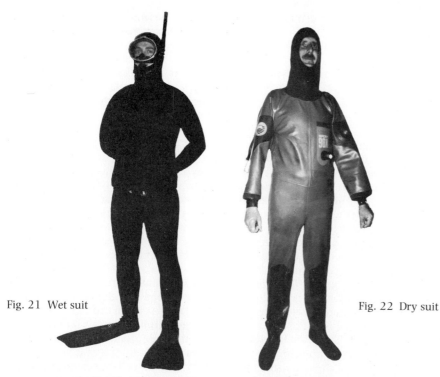

Fig. 21 Wet suit

Fig. 22 Dry suit

In order to increase the strength of the wet suit against tearing, most are made from a nylon-lined material. However, care must still be taken to avoid catching them on sharp projections or rocks.

Another type of suit that may be worn by divers – particularly in very cold waters – is the **dry suit** (Fig. 22). This suit is made as a thin rubberised membrane with seals at the ankles, wrists, and at the hood around the face. The diver enters the suit through a waterproof zip across the shoulders. Protection from the cold is obtained by wearing woollen or other special warm clothing inside the suit. Proper training is necessary before diving with these suits and they are not recommended for beginners.

Lifejackets
There is a special adjustable buoyancy lifejacket for divers – known as an ABLJ (Fig. 23). Not only can it bring a diver up from depth in an emergency and then support him and his equipment at the surface, but it can also be used by the diver to adjust his buoyancy while under water.

water compresses the bubbles within the material of the suit and its buoyancy will decrease. This loss of buoyancy may be quite large on deeper dives and the diver must make allowances for it by taking less weight, otherwise he may have difficulties in making his ascent.

Fig. 23 Adjustable buoyancy lifejacket (ABLJ)

Before a dive it is essential to fill the small cylinder in the lifejacket with air from a charged aqualung cylinder. The lifejacket should be put on before other equipment so that, if necessary, the aqualung and weightbelt can be removed while still in the water, leaving the lifejacket in place.

The buoyancy of a diver's wet suit will decrease as he descends, but he can compensate for this by letting a small amount of air into his lifejacket. In order to prevent too rapid an ascent the diver must vent off this air in a controlled manner by using a cord operated 'dump valve'.

Lifejackets are usually fitted with a special mouthpiece that performs the combined functions of venting, oral inflation at the surface, and the possibility of breathing air from the lifejacket in an emergency (Fig. 24). There

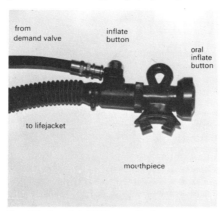

Fig. 24 Special ABLJ mouthpiece

is sometimes also a 'direct feed' inflator which is connected to a medium pressure take off on the diver's demand valve.

This type of lifejacket has many advantages for the diver, but its special features should only be used after thorough and careful training.

Preliminary training

Although diving with an aqualung is easy, it can be very hazardous if not done properly. The surest way to learn how to do this is to have a sound training, commencing if possible in the safe waters of a swimming pool. Apart from knowing how the equipment works, the beginner should familiarise himself with its functioning by assembling it and testing it personally. After learning how to put on and fit the harness, adjust the weights for neutral buoyancy and having become accustomed to finning and breathing from the aqualung under water, certain safety drills should be practised and mastered.

Should water get into the mask it can be cleared out without the need to surface. While vertical in the water, tilt the head upwards, place one hand on the top of the mask to keep it firmly on the forehead and breathe out through the nose (Fig. 25). The water will then be driven out at the bottom of the mask. A further attempt can be made when necessary. This drill should be practised by first letting a little water into the bottom of the mask and clearing it out. Repeat this letting in more and more water each time until it is possible to take the mask completely off under water, refit and clear it satisfactorily. Even if using a mask which incorporates a drain valve to assist clearing, it is still necessary to master this drill.

The methods of clearing water from the mouthpiece should be practised in an upright position and later while finning horizontally. When replacing the mouthpiece, depressing the purge button will give a steady supply of air (Fig. 26), but if you have retained suffi- cient air in your lungs it is possible to clear water from the demand valve by exhalation alone. If you are unable to replace the mouthpiece and breathe normally again, it is most important never to surface holding your breath, but to rise slowly, breathing out as you go.

The third drill which should be mastered is changing over from aqualung to snorkel tube on surfacing. Even though breathing from the aqualung keep the snorkel tube fitted at the side of the mask, on the opposite side from the demand valve hose. When ready to change over to snorkel breathing take a full breath, remove the demand valve mouthpiece with one hand and hold it downwards in the water; at the same time move the snorkel mouthpiece with the other hand to fit it into your mouth. Keeping your face in the water, clear the snorkel with a strong blow. Do this at the surface, first while standing in water just up to your neck and later while finning in deeper water. Mastering this drill enable you to change over to snorkel safely if a surface fin is necessary at the end of a dive.

Fig. 25 Clearing the mask

Fig. 26 Clearing the mouthpiece

Sea diving

Of paramount importance – particularly with an aqualung – is **never to dive alone**. This safety rule should always be observed; dive with a companion and keep with him at all times both under the water and on the surface. An accident in diving can be fatal as drowning can occur in only a few seconds. In times of emergency the immediate assistance of your companion diver – or of you to him – may prove vital.

Before entering the water you should adopt the practice of making a regular series of pre-dive checks, which will depend to some extent on the equipment you are using. First, check that you have all your essential equipment and any special items you may be requiring for the dive (Fig. 27). Check the important items in turn: the mask correctly fitted, fins on and secure, that you have a snorkel tube for use on the surface, and a lifejacket. See that the aqualung harness is correctly adjusted and that you have sufficient buoyancy

weights. Then check your air supply by attempting to inhale with the air turned off – there should be no leaks in the system. Turn on the air and you should be able to breathe freely – check the pressure gauge or air reserve valve if you have one, to see the amount of air in the cylinder. If everything is correct feel for the quick-release of your weights to see that you can operate it without difficulty and that the weights will fall away freely. Check your companion diver and you are ready to dive.

When entering the water from the shore wade out backwards if the water is clear, or else climb carefully over any rocks or obstructions until you are able to fin away. On leaving the water at a rocky coastline keep your face in the water in order to see where you can safely go.

It is important to know what factors limit the depth to which you should dive. These are: the depth of water in which you are diving, your ability to clear your ears satisfactorily, the time

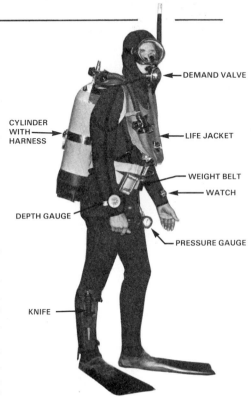

DEMAND VALVE

CYLINDER WITH HARNESS

LIFE JACKET

WEIGHT BELT

WATCH

DEPTH GAUGE

PRESSURE GAUGE

KNIFE

Fig. 27 The properly equipped sea diver

25

you can stay below due to the limited amount of air in your cylinders, and the dangers of 'nitrogen narcosis' and the 'bends'. There should be no difficulty at all for dives to a depth of 10 metres and, when the diver has gained sufficient experience, very little for dives of limited duration down to 30 metres.

The duration of a dive depends on three factors: the amount of air in your cylinders, your breathing rate and the depth at which you are diving. This last results from the necessity to breathe air at the pressure of the surrounding water. In order to take the same volume into the lungs, twice the mass of air is used at a depth of 10 metres as it is at the surface and in consequence the air in the cylinders will last for only half the time, with corresponding variations at other depths.

Probably the most dangerous time for a diver is on surfacing at the end of a dive. Tired or cold, encumbered by heavy equipment, with his air supply possibly low or exhausted and maybe in a choppy sea, he can soon get into difficulties if a proper surfacing drill is not carried out. This drill should be

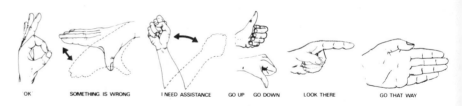

Fig. 28 Underwater signals

learnt and practised until it becomes almost instinctive. When starting the ascent, feel for the weight quick-release, in case it should be needed. On nearing the surface prepare to change over from aqualung to snorkel tube, either by fitting the tube behind the mask strap and holding it in the hand ready to insert in the mouth, or by placing your hand on the tube if it is already fixed to the mask. On breaking surface take one last breath from the aqualung, change over to snorkel and clear it with a strong blow. You are now able to continue on the surface, using the snorkel without the need for an air supply from the cylinder. For this reason **a snorkel tube is essential** and should always be taken with you on a dive. If you wish to increase your buoy-

ancy at the surface you can then partially inflate your lifejacket.

On surfacing at the end of a dive, you and your companion should come up together, so at once look to see that everything is all right with him. Then look around to find your direction or the point from which you started the dive.

When diving in low visibility waters or in strong currents the divers should be attached to a rope which is under the charge of a competent person on land or boat. Signals can be given by pulls on the rope between the diver and his attendant. The diver should always carry a knife in such circumstances to cut himself free in case he should become snagged by the rope. In currents it is safer to commence by finning up current and then allow it to carry you back to your point of entry at the end of the dive.

Diver signals

It is difficult to communicate under water. However, a system of mutually understood signals can be used to convey essential information (Fig. 28). O.K. is given by a round 'O' made by finger and thumb of one hand. Something wrong is shown by rocking the open hand, while moving the clenched fist from side to side means assistance is needed. Indicating 'up' and 'down' is done with the thumb, and direction by the flat hand, Drawing attention to another person or object is done by pointing with the forefinger. All these signals can be used either for question or answer and they should invariably be answered by an appropriate signal.

Another set of signals should be used at the surface between the divers and those on the shore or in the boat (Fig. 29). These signals are: 'O.K.' – one arm held straight upwards with fingers and thumb formed into an O, or 'I need assistance' – by waving one arm fully in an arc from side to side. These signals

Fig. 29 Surface signals

should be answered and action taken by the surface party lookout, who should at all times have been following the divers' progress by watching for their exhaust bubbles or by other means. Divers who have surfaced should not dive again unless the surface party lookout signals to them that it is O.K. for them to do so.

Other equipment

Besides his aqualung, fins, mask and snorkel the diver will often have need to carry other equipment. Diving suits and lifejackets are of considerable importance and are mentioned separately.

To know the depth attained during a dive is important so as to give an indication of the distance for surfacing and

how long the diver can remain safely under water. A depth gauge (Fig. 30) is a necessity if going more than a few metres below the surface. The simple open-ended tube type may be considered satisfactory for shallow dives, but for safety on deeper ones an accurate gauge with a pointer and scale should be used. It is also desirable that the gauge retains an indication of the maximum depth reached on the dive.

A waterproof watch (Fig. 31) is necessary on deeper dives to check the duration under water and time for surfacing. It should be specially made

Fig. 30 Depth gauge

Fig. 31 Underwater watch

to withstand the pressures (which an ordinary waterproof watch will not do), and it is an advantage if it is fitted with an adjustable time duration scale.

You can find your way about under water by observing nearby objects in line with each other, noting the positions of rocks and patches of seaweed, or even by detecting the direction of current flow as shown by the movement of weed and the drift of suspended matter in the water. However, a useful addition to your equipment is a compass (Fig. 32) for finding direction in waters of poor visibility, or to fin on a particular course under water. Quite a simple one will do. Care should be taken to keep it as far away as possible from steel aqualung cylinders which will influence the compass reading.

Holding it well out in front of you is the most suitable position.

There is a useful console for divers which combines in one unit the pressure gauge with a compass and depth timer (Fig. 33). When the diver enters the water this timer starts to record the dive time and depth reached.

A diver's knife (Fig. 34) in a plastic or metal sheath is very useful and should always be carried if diving with ropes. It should have one plain and one serrated edge and may be fitted either at the diver's waist or to one of his legs.

An underwater torch (Fig. 35) is useful in dark waters or when diving within wrecks or below rocks. It can also be used to enable the diver to see the true colours of objects in deeper water where natural light has been reduced to shades of green or grey.

Diver's flag

A diver on the surface or below the water cannot be seen easily by ships and other users of the diving area. It is therefore advisable to avoid diving where surface craft are present. The diver's position can be indicated, however, by flying the International Code

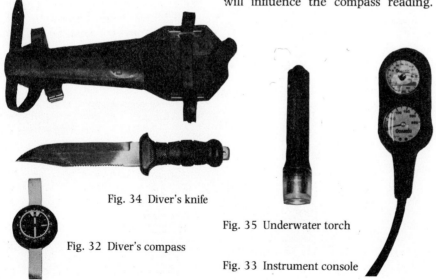

Fig. 34 Diver's knife

Fig. 32 Diver's compass

Fig. 35 Underwater torch

Fig. 33 Instrument console

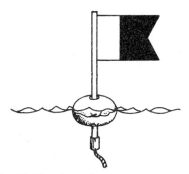

Fig. 36 Diver's marker buoy

flag 'A' – a white and blue flag – which is used to denote that 'divers are down'. Although this will not give automatic protection or obviate the need to take care when or where you dive, it is a signal which can be recognised by shipping and should be flown as an added safety precaution.

Small marker buoys are available carrying a diver's flag, attached by a light floating line to a reel held by the diver (Fig. 36). They serve the dual purpose of warning surface craft that a diver is immediately below and also of pinpointing the diver's position to his surface party. They are very useful when drift diving in a current.

Boat diving

With the growing popularity of underwater swimming, an increasing number of people go aqualung diving from a boat. This enables them to go further afield in search of good diving sites and to get away from crowded beaches and murky inshore waters. Generally small boats are used which can carry several pairs of divers and their equipment (Fig. 37).

It is not the purpose of this book to explain the use of small boats, the effects of tides and currents or the methods of coastal navigation, but every diver who owns a boat should be fully conversant with these matters and competent in handling it correctly.

Fig. 37 Diver's boat

When at the diving site never leave the boat unattended, and ensure that it is properly anchored – the rope should be about 3 times the depth of the water. When the boat has settled and the anchor is firm the engine should be cut; divers should never be in the water while the propeller is still turning. The ideal entry to the water is from a special diving ladder. From a small boat, however, an effective method is to sit on the side and allow yourself to roll in backwards, retaining your mask in position with one hand as you enter the water. Once in the water check with your companion that you are both all right. For the dive it is an advantage to descend holding on to the anchor rope as this makes it easier for ear clearing and prevents drifting astern of the boat on the way down. On reaching the seabed it is preferable to fin up current.

A lookout should always be kept from the boat for the divers surfacing. When they reach the side they should be helped on board. It may be preferable for them to remove their equipment in the water before entering the boat. The boat should not leave the diving site until all the divers have returned.

Diving dangers

There are a number of problems and hazards associated with diving, of which all divers should be aware. You should know when these hazards are likely to arise, learn how to avoid them, and if they should occur be able to take the correct action to prevent their becoming a serious danger to yourself or your companion diver.

The risk of trouble increases with deeper dives, in waters of poor visibility, and in currents. Such diving should only be undertaken by adequately experienced divers, after careful preparation, and with proper surface support.

Sea creatures

Generally the diver has little to fear from attack by sea creatures. As on land, most will shy away from man to hide or shelter. Of course, there are exceptions such as some species of shark that will attack, particularly if the diver is making rapid movements like a fish in distress. Then there are certain tropical water creatures that can injure a diver, such as the lionfish whose spines carry a virulent poison, stinging coral that produces a painful burn when in contact with the skin, and some jellyfish whose tentacles may reach far below them. In colder waters danger only comes by disturbing or deliberate provocation such as attempting to catch crabs or lobsters whose claws can effect a damaging crush. In these waters the main problem comes from scratches and cuts on jagged rocks, barnacles, and sharp metal on wrecks. Sensible precautions and behaviour will reduce even these to small risks.

Exhaustion

One of the greatest dangers to a diver is exhaustion. It can be brought about in many ways: continued heavy exertion, repeated diving, long exposure to cold or even a short time in very cold conditions, overtiredness, lack of food, poor physical condition, diving over-weighted, long finning on the surface wearing an aqualung or finning in heavy seas, and panic.

The onset of exhaustion can be very sudden, although sometimes a feeling of physical or mental tiredness is a preliminary warning. In such cases the dive should be terminated and the diver leave the water. This may be possible if he has an adequate supply of air, but in many of the circumstances where exhaustion occurs there is little air available. Most cases of drowning are preceded by exhaustion, if only that produced in frantically fighting to keep the head above water.

Accordingly the diver should take special care to avoid the risk of exhaustion by carefully planning his dive and carrying it out sensibly. Above all, he should prepare himself to deal with it effectively should it occur. The surest means is to wear a lifejacket and to inflate it without delay before the exhaustion has become extreme. When diving **always wear a lifejacket**.

Burst lungs

There are a number of diving hazards that are associated with the use of an aqualung, which are due to the increase and variations of pressure acting on the diver as he changes his depth in the water. Should he hold his breath and ascend, as the water pressure decreases, the air in the diver's lungs will expand; and should he continue for even a few metres the expanding air will damage the air sacs in the lungs and possibly enter the blood where it will form bubbles. These bubbles may easily restrict the blood flow to some vital part of the body and cause the condition known as 'air embolism' which is very dangerous and may well prove fatal. Its most severe

Fig. 38 Waiting for the diving boat

symptoms are blood at the mouth, pain in the chest and unconsciousness. The only treatment is recompression under medical supervision as soon as possible to reduce the size of the bubbles.

Trouble from lung damage will not occur if the diver breathes normally at all times, as any changes of pressure are compensated for at each breath. Hence it is extremely important when diving, and especially when surfacing, to **never hold your breath when using an aqualung**.

Lung damage is especially liable to occur in the event of the diver making an emergency ascent, if perhaps the air supply has failed or a lifejacket has been used from depth. In such a case the diver should exhale continuously on the way up to avoid the risk of excess pressure of air in the lungs.

Nitrogen narcosis

Although nitrogen performs no active part in respiration at normal air pressures, as the diver goes deeper, with the consequent increase in the pressure of the air, the nitrogen gradually produces an effect similar to drunkenness, which is called 'nitrogen narcosis'.

Down to depths of about 30 metres the effect is slight but as the diver goes deeper his senses and judgement will be impaired until he becomes a danger to himself and his companion through his inability to think clearly and concentrate on his diving. At 50 metres the effects may be quite pronounced. They will vary considerably from one diver to another and from day to day. The most dangerous effects of the onset of nitrogen narcosis are overconfidence and a lack of the warning signs of fear. As these usually come on quite slowly, the diver has always to be alert otherwise he may not be aware of them until they are severe.

On rising towards the surface the effects of nitrogen narcosis diminish and disappear, and leave no aftereffects so they can be overcome if recognised in time. A diver should build up his diving experience gradually towards the deeper dives. However, for safety, deep dives should be avoided. It is foolish to make them for their own sake, and anyway, by far the most interesting and abundant underwater life is to be found in the first 30 metres of depth.

The bends

As the diver descends he breathes air at a pressure equal to that of the surrounding water. Nitrogen in the air at this pressure is taken up by the blood and starts to saturate the tissues of the body. The amount absorbed depends on the time the diver has been below as well as the depth at which he is diving. This extra nitrogen is quite harmless in itself and in the ordinary course of events; as the diver ascends again, it will come out of solution in the tissues and escape the way it went in – via the blood and lungs.

If, however, the diver exceeds certain limits of depth and duration of dive and then ascends at too great a rate, nitrogen will come out of solution too fast to be carried away by the blood and bubbles may form in the tissues, giving rise to pains and other troubles known to divers as 'the bends', but medically termed 'decompression sickness'. The effects of decompression sickness can be quite severe, possibly causing permanent paralysis or even death.

In order to avoid 'the bends' the diver must make his ascent sufficiently slowly to let the excess nitrogen get away. If he has been down for sufficient time at any particular depth it may even be necessary for him to rest at certain depths on the way up, to allow more time for the nitrogen to escape. This process is called making 'decompression stops'.

If the diver has not been deeper than 9 metres there is no need for decompression. Even for greater depths if the time of the dive has been limited the ascent can be made without stops, provided it is done at the slow rate of about 15 metres a minute. This speed of ascent corresponds approximately to the speed at which the small bubbles from the diver's exhalations rise to the surface. For this reason – and also as an added precaution against the risk of air embolism – the diver should **always ascend at the rate of the small bubbles**.

Although a severe attack of 'the bends', calls for recompression under expert medical attention as soon as possible, a mild one may be felt as local pain in one joint only, which may pass off after a short time. However, even with a mild 'bend' medical advice should be sought.

Decompression tables

In order to obviate risks of 'the bends', tables of decompression have been prepared for dives of different duration and depths giving the stops necessary on the ascent. Sufficient air must be allowed in the dive planning to make the stops. When calculating decompression requirements from these tables, the maximum depth attained on the dive must be used, even if you only stayed at it for a short time; the duration of the dive is from leaving the surface until commencing the final ascent. Decompression stops can be quite difficult to perform. If diving from a boat, a practical way of doing them is to hold on to the anchor rope. However, this can be an unpleasant process if the boat is riding on a swell, the water is cold, or you are tired at the end of the dive.

On leaving the water after a dive some time must elapse for the diver to be rid of the excess nitrogen from the body tissues. There is thus an added complication if more than one dive is done in one day. If a second dive is made below 9 metres it is necessary also to take into account the depth and duration of the first dive for determining decompression requirements.

Dives needing decompression stops should only be undertaken after adequate training and with proper dive organisation. Owing to these complications aqualung divers are recommended to avoid dives or repeat dives that involve decompression stops on the ascent. If using a 'decompression meter', divers must still take great care over their decompression.

Maximum duration of a single dive for an ascent without decompression stops

DEPTH (metres)	MINUTES
Surface	No limit
5	No limit
9	No limit
15	70
20	45
25	30
30	20
35	14
40	11
45	8
50	7

Care of equipment

All underwater swimming equipment needs proper care and attention, particularly as not only your enjoyment but also your life may depend on its correct functioning. Most of the maintenance can be done by the diver himself. Equipment made of rubber, fins, masks, diving suits, will perish if left exposed to the sun or salt water. They should be washed in fresh water after use and left to dry. If they will not be used for some time they should be dusted with french chalk to prevent sticking and stored in a cool, dry place until next required. Other items should be washed after use and dried.

Harnesses should be repaired if worn and weight belts checked to ensure that the quick-release mechanism is in order.

Unless you are specially qualified only limited attention can be given to such things as cylinders, demand valves and lifejackets, which should be washed as other items, but otherwise returned to the makers for overhaul or repair whenever this is necessary.

Diving suits require special attention. After each use they should be thoroughly washed in fresh water both for hygienic reasons and to remove deposits of salt or mud. They should be allowed to dry naturally and any nicks or tears should be repaired with a suitable adhesive. To avoid deterioration they should be stored away from heat or exposure to the sun.

The success and enjoyment of a dive will depend on proper preparation of equipment beforehand; this should not be left until the moment of departure. If requisite maintenance and repairs have previously been carried out it should only be necessary to give attention to the specific needs of the forthcoming dive by ensuring that the aqualung cylinder is fully charged with air, all normal diving equipment is gathered together and packed, along with any items specifically required for that particular dive, such as underwater camera and film.

Lifesaving

Drowning is unfortunately only too easy an occurrence and everyone who takes part in water activities should become competent in methods of lifesaving. A diver is far better able to attempt the rescue of someone in distress as he has the advantage of the power of his fins and of his other equipment. Special methods of rescue and lifesaving have been developed by the British Sub-Aqua Club and the Royal Life Saving Society, which divers should learn during their training. It is important not to attempt a rescue if in the process you may yourself become a casualty.

Fig. 39 Towing with fins

Rescue towing

Only a few seconds may elapse between a person getting into difficulties and drowning. To render effective assistance, therefore, no time should be lost in getting to him, where necessary bringing him to the surface, and supporting him in the water. Towing a victim is very strenuous and, if possible, summon assistance of a boat or another rescuer.

If the victim is struggling at the surface, the rescuer should approach him from behind so as to avoid his clutch, then hold him firmly and keep his head above water. If the victim is a fully equipped diver it will help to inflate his lifejacket and perhaps also to remove his weight belt and aqualung.

When towing, grip the victim's chin and if added support is required place the other hand under his neck. The rescuer should fin at one side or below the victim for the most effective towing (Fig. 39).

Artificial respiration

In the event of apparent drowning where breathing has ceased, artificial respiration should always be tried without delay.

Expired Air Resuscitation is the most satisfactory method to use. First ensure that the victim's air passages are clear; water may be drained out by placing him on his side, head downwards. Then lay the victim on his back and

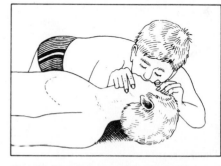

Fig. 40 Mouth to mouth resuscitation

apply mouth-to-mouth resuscitation; with one hand tilt the head backwards and squeeze the nose, with the other hand push the jaw upwards to prevent the tongue from blocking the airways. Take a normal breath and place your mouth over his. Breathe out – so that your exhaled air flows into his lungs and his chest rises. Remove your mouth and breathe in, during which

Fig. 41 Mouth to nose resuscitation in the water

time the victim's lungs should deflate of their own accord. Replace your mouth over his and continue as before (Fig. 40).

With adequate training it is possible to give Expired Air Resuscitation while still in the water. In this case the victim is held and towed by placing one hand in the nape of the neck to keep his head above water. The other hand holds the chin and tilts back the head while at the same time the thumb is used to seal off the victim's mouth. The rescuer should apply mouth-to-nose resuscitation by turning the victim's face towards him in the water and exhaling into his lungs through the nose (Fig. 41).

If after a few breaths the victim shows no signs of recovery or return of colour to the cheeks, his heart may have stopped beating. If no pulse can be felt and the rescuer is competent to give 'external chest compression', this should be applied alternately with the expired air resuscitation.

Always summon help and medical aid even if the victim appears to have regained normal breathing.

Diving activities

The majority of people who take up diving do so to explore a new, alien, and fascinating world. A diver experiences significant changes to his senses; vision is restricted, light dims, colours fade; sound is all but gone and its direction cannot be determined; touch responds to the cold, wetness and resistance of the water which is everywhere – pressing on him as he descends, supporting his whole body and producing the sensations of weightlessness.

Because of this strangeness it is necessary to make a conscious effort at observation to see and identify the surroundings, the type of seabed, plants and creatures seen on the dive. It is a great help to your appreciation and enjoyment of diving if you consult reference books on life in the sea so that you can recognise things and learn about them. It also helps you to discuss the details of your dives afterwards with other divers.

With experience the diver learns to be at home in the underwater world.

He may then, if he wishes, devote some of his diving to specific activities such as archaeological exploration of wrecks, undersea geology, or scientific studies of marine life. To do this he may have to learn new subjects and techniques thereby deriving much interest, personal satisfaction and an added purpose in his diving.

Underwater photography

Taking underwater photographs is a most rewarding aspect of underwater swimming, but because of the limited amount of light, poor visibility, lack of contrast and movement of the diver by the water much care and patience is required to develop the skills necessary to get good pictures.

In general the techniques for getting a good picture are similar to taking photographs on land, but there are a number of special factors that also have to be taken into account. Firstly, a suitable waterproof camera case is required that makes provision for operation of the essential controls while

Fig. 42 Underwater camera

under water. The simpler the operation of the camera the better. Probably the best is a self-contained camera (Fig. 42) designed to be used under water; alternatively a special waterproof housing can be used with a camera. Due to the magnification effect of viewing under water – similar to that experienced by the diver when looking through his face mask – a wide angle lens is to be

preferred, otherwise only a small area – probably less than that necessary to show a complete diver – can be got into the picture.

When light passes through water its intensity is rapidly reduced and a colour filtering effect also takes place, which diminishes first the red colours, followed by the yellows and leaving shades of green and blue (Fig. 43), which give the sea its characteristic colour. This must be taken into account when taking a photograph under water. In consequence the best photographs can be taken just below the surface in strong sunlight. As a rough guide, in clear water when just below the surface the camera lens should be opened up 3 or 4 stops more than for a photograph above the water. Increase the lens aperture by 1 extra stop for each increase of 3 metres in depth. Contrast under water is usually poor and therefore better results are obtained by taking contrasting subjects, for example, fish, rocks, or seaweed against a light background of sand in a depth of less than 6 metres.

At depths where much of the colour of natural light has gone it is possible to

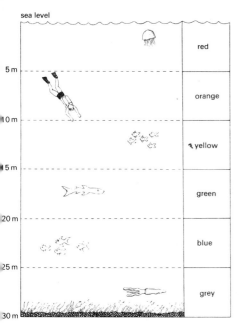

sea level

red

5 m

orange

10 m

yellow

15 m

green

20 m

blue

25 m

grey

30 m

Fig. 43 Colour absorption at depth

restore this to the photograph by use of a waterproofed flash attachment to the underwater camera. However, due to the strong absorption of light by the water the effective range of flash is reduced to 1 or 2 metres.

Wrecks

Most divers experience a thrill when coming upon a wreck under water. It is not the lure of sunken treasure, nor the prospect of gaining a personal trophy such as a brass porthole, but the presence of something man-made, in which man once lived and sailed, now destroyed, deserted and forgotten. The real fascination of a wreck, however, is not its past, but the wealth of marine life which now inhabits it. Taken over by the sea, it provides a strong anchorage for seaweed, a safe haven for fish to swim and congregate in its cabins and holds, for crabs and lobsters to lurk in corners and under protective ledges, a shelter where sea anemones and sponges can grow.

But not all wrecks resemble their former ships. Those inshore are usually broken up by waves and scattered as debris among rocks, buried below sand or mud, or blown up wherever they might have been a danger to shipping. Only a wreck which lies in fairly deep water well clear of shore is likely to be relatively intact and recognisable as a former ship (Fig. 44).

Fig. 44 Wreck encrusted with coral

Because of the danger of running out of breath, snorkel divers should not venture inside a wreck and even when using an aqualung such action can be perilous. It is quite easy to get lost inside, particularly where fine silt, which settles below decks, becomes stirred up by divers' fins. Rusted steel plates are liable to collapse and their sharp, torn edges can cause deep cuts.

All wrecks belong to someone, or are of archaeological interest, so you should never take anything from one without permission.

Underwater archaeology

Much of the heritage of the past is preserved in the buried towns round the coastline where the land has subsided and in the wrecks of ships from ancient times. The Nautical Archaeological Society has been established to research and record sites of underwater historical interest. Much work of this nature has already been done and divers contribute significantly to it.

Marine conservation

The greatest enjoyment for most divers is observing the marine life in its own natural environment. In doing this it is a great help to know the names of the various common seaweeds and animals which inhabit the different areas of the sea and different depths. Where the sea is over exploited by fishing, damage is done to that environment and plants, fish and animals die. Even the limited activities of divers can affect the presence of certain species that inhabit specific regions. In Britain the Marine Conservation Society has been established to help divers get to know the underwater world, to appreciate its beauty and to help preserve it from destruction.

Competitions

Spearfishing as a sport is now less popular than it used to be as divers have turned to other interests underwater, while in some countries it is illegal or a spearfishing licence is required. Competitions are usually

Fig. 45 Photographing marine life

confined to snorkel divers; they are strictly controlled for safety, as spearguns are lethal weapons.

Octopush, which is a form of underwater hockey with two teams of players, has become popular in Britain. A league has been set up and some international games are played. It is a strenuous snorkelling activity with some specialist clubs catering only for this sport.

Fin swimming as a competitive sport is popular in some countries. Competitors use fins much larger than those for normal diving purposes. The race may be held in a swimming pool or in open water.

Underwater orienteering involves competing around a set course underwater by the use of compass and other instruments. It relies on very precise navigation and the results are judged on both the speed and accuracy of completing the course.

Diving qualifications

The following BSAC diving qualifications (which are also recognised internationally by the World Federation of Sub-Aqua Activities – CMAS) are awarded to members by their branch of the Club:

Novice diver
A diver who is competent in the safe and correct use of all appropriate open-water aqualung diving equipment in a sheltered-water training area and is ready to gain open-water diving experience in the company of a dive leader or more highly qualified diver/instructor.

Sports diver (CMAS two-star diver)
A diver who has gained some open-water diving experience and is considered ready to take part in dives partnered by a diver of the same, or higher, grade. A sports diver would not have sufficient experience to take a novice diver on open-water dives.

Dive leader
An active, experienced and responsible diver, competent in dive leadership, who may lead others on open-water dives.

Advanced diver (CMAS three-star diver)
A fully trained and responsible diver who is competent to organise and lead branch diving activities.

Nationally awarded qualifications

First-class diver (CMAS four-star diver)
An advanced diver who has attained a higher than average level of knowledge and ability, assessed through nationally conducted examinations and able to utilise divers and diving in order to achieve major tasks or project objectives.

Fig. 46 International diver's card

Divers' code

Diving is a wonderful sport, full of fascination and achievement. Thousands have now tasted its thrills, but in their enthusiasm there may be some people who disregard the fact that there are other users of the baths, the sea or the diving sites. Irresponsible and inconsiderate actions can give any sport a bad name and divers should take particular care to enhance the reputation of their sport by considerate behaviour. By keeping to the following Divers' Code you will achieve this.

1. Do not impede or interfere with other swimmers or divers.

2. Always obey the instructions of local officials, harbour masters, swimming bath authorities.

3. Do not dive in private waters or go on to private land without the owner's permission.

4. Do not obstruct roads or public places or cause a nuisance with your vehicles or diving equipment.

5. Do not dive in 'fairways'; and fly the Divers' Flag whenever divers are in the water.

6. Do not interfere with fishermen or their equipment; or with the activities of other users of the diving area.

7. Do not use a speargun near swimmers or fishermen; or in fresh waters. Never load it out of the water.

8. Do not take fish or shellfish below the minimum permitted sizes; or anything from wrecks without permission.

Join a club

The importance of companion diving is obvious. Unless you are already associated with a number of other divers by far the best way to meet some is to join a reputable diving club. Not only will this give you the chance to go diving, but you will make diving friends, and be able to join with them on diving outings to sea or lakes. There will be opportunity for you to train and learn your diving techniques in safety and under competent guidance; and you in your turn will be able to help other beginners to the sport. Many clubs have cylinder-charging facilities and own a number of the more expensive items of equipment such as aqualungs and inflatable boats for the use of their members.

By going through a course of training you can become qualified as a sports diver. The British Sub-Aqua Club has over 1,000 branches in the United Kingdom and in other parts of the world for aqualung diving, and also over 200 branches of its Snorkellers Club which cater mainly for junior divers prior to their reaching the age to use an aqualung. Standard training procedures are used so that training and diving qualifications obtained in any branch are recognised throughout the country and by many diving organisations abroad. This is most useful when you travel or go on holiday as you are able to produce acceptable evidence of your diving ability. For full details and lists of local branches write to:

THE BRITISH SUB-AQUA CLUB
16 Upper Woburn Place, London
WC1H 0QW.